CELEBRATING THE FAMILY NAME OF BURNS

Celebrating the Family Name of Burns

Walter the Educator

Silent King Books
a WhichHead Entertainment Imprint

Copyright © 2024 by Walter the Educator

All rights reserved. No part of this book may be reproduced in any manner whatsoever without written permission except in the case of brief quotations embodied in critical articles and reviews.

First Printing, 2024

Disclaimer

This book is a literary work; the story is not about specific persons, locations, situations, and/or circumstances unless mentioned in a historical context. Any resemblance to real persons, locations, situations, and/or circumstances is coincidental. This book is for entertainment and informational purposes only. The author and publisher offer this information without warranties expressed or implied. No matter the grounds, neither the author nor the publisher will be accountable for any losses, injuries, or other damages caused by the reader's use of this book. The use of this book acknowledges an understanding and acceptance of this disclaimer.

Celebrating the Family Name of Burns is a memory book that belongs to the Celebrating Family Name Book Series by Walter the Educator. Collect them all and more books at WaltertheEducator.com

USE THE EXTRA SPACE TO DOCUMENT YOUR FAMILY MEMORIES THROUGHOUT THE YEARS

BURNS

The name of Burns, like flames that glow,

Celebrating the Family Name of

Burns

A spark ignites where'er they go.

In hearts and minds, in dreams and deeds,

The Burns' legacy forever leads.

Through ancient lands, where rivers wind,

A family born of fire and mind,

With eyes that gleam and spirits bright,

The Burns clan walks with boundless light.

Their name, a torch against the night,

A beacon bold, forever bright.

In fields of green, in cities wide,

The name of Burns stands dignified.

From humble roots, the fire was kindled,

A flame that never once has dwindled.

In every soul, a steady blaze,

That lights their path in countless ways.

Celebrating the Family Name of

Burns

With every tale, with every rhyme,

They burn with passion through all time.

Through winds of change, through storm and strife,

Burns' strength endures, a flame of life.

A name that speaks of fierce desire,

To rise above, to climb, aspire.

The Burns pursue with steady grace,

A noble heart in every place.

In fields of art, in realms of thought,

The Burns with brilliance have always fought.

They stoke the embers of the mind,

A flame of truth, a light refined.

Each generation builds anew,

A legacy both bold and true.

With every spark, the fire grows,

Through every season, through every rose.

The Burns know well that life's a dance,

A fleeting flame, a fleeting chance.

But in their hearts, the fire remains,

Through all of life's uncertain gains.

Celebrating the Family Name of

Burns

Their laughter crackles like the fire,

Their voices rise, their spirits higher.

For in the Burns, the warmth is real,

A family flame you always feel.

ABOUT THE CREATOR

Walter the Educator is one of the pseudonyms for Walter Anderson. Formally educated in Chemistry, Business, and Education, he is an educator, an author, a diverse entrepreneur, and he is the son of a disabled war veteran. "Walter the Educator" shares his time between educating and creating. He holds interests and owns several creative projects that entertain, enlighten, enhance, and educate, hoping to inspire and motivate you. Follow, find new works, and stay up to date with Walter the Educator™

at WaltertheEducator.com

www.ingramcontent.com/pod-product-compliance
Lightning Source LLC
LaVergne TN
LVHW010622070526
838199LV00063BA/5232